I am that I am

I am the wind
and you are the fire
I like to fly with you
high and higher

I am the sun,
the moon and the stars
I will see you soon
it's not very far

My spirit is rising
my heart is light
when we meet again
everything will be allright

es tanzen im Mondlicht
die Hexen der Nacht
haben es weit, sehr weit -
bis zu den Engeln gebracht
tanzen jetzt im frohen Reigen
werden sich dir selten zeigen
sind Energie und Licht und Glück
denn sie blicken nie zurück.

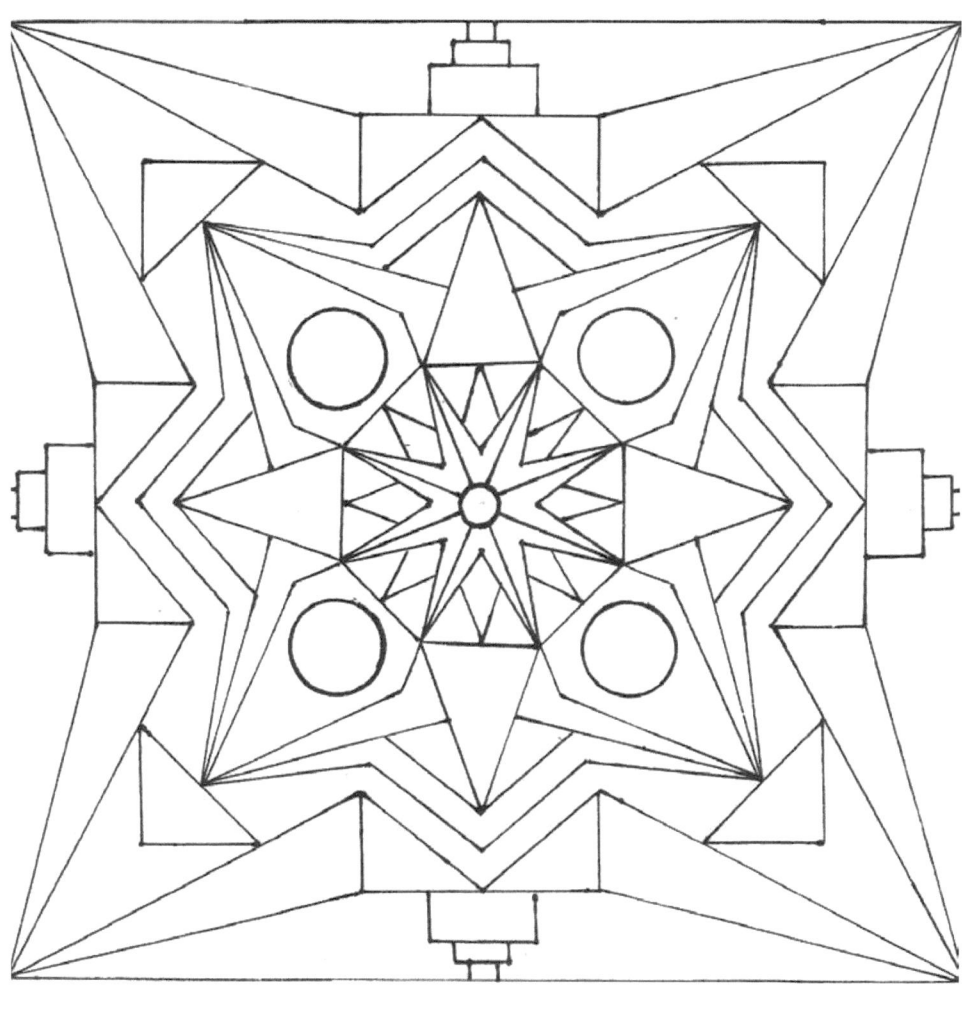

You're Frozen when your heart is not open

you live in this world so serious and cold
nowhere to touch you that can give me a hold
you're wasting your time with your frozen heart
right now we seem to be light-years apart

let me melt your heart
then we'll never be apart
we''ll walk a road unknown before
nothing to hold on to - just a big open door
at the end when laughter will cease
we'll be in the light and feel the peace

two strangers we are in a world so cold
should we not be daring and bold
lift our spirits high into the air
could we - should we - really dare

on a silvery beam of a star very bright
the elfs are dancing in an eerie night
they are turning and laughing and giggling out loud
do you know what they are talking about

the picture is torn the world is broken
we feel we have used our very last token
HE just t knows and we reach for His hand
we never left where we now and forever will end

grauer himmel, keine sorgen
keine freude, nur viel stille
über den wolken der blaue himmel
vergiss das nicht
darunter bist du doch geborgen

darüber sind engel
die lachen mit dir
die kennen nicht tränen
die sind einfach hier

die stille ist einfach
sie ist einfach und schön
fühle es
dann kannst du auch sehn

do I know who I am
do I really know?
is life just show after show
do I really care to know?

maybe I am here, maybe I am not
everything is upside down and feels like a knot
maybe I know you, maybe I don´t
maybe I should guess, maybe I won´t.

my life feels empty now and sad
and I don´t know if this is good or bad
am really tired of thinking in vain
just stop this and begin to gain

gain momentum in a world fast and slow
everything is tense and we want to grow
if we grow where do we want to go
I´ll just be quiet and try not to say no.

no is not much, but it has to be said
somehow it moves you miles ahead
ahead and back it´s all the same
let´s listen and learn it´s all a game

Engel schweben in freiem Licht
sie fliegen von dir zu mir
und zurück wieder zu dir
und sind Träger von Harmonie,
Liebe und einer neuen Sicht.

Die silbrige Schnur zwischen dir und mir
bestätigt sich immer im jetzt und hier
Reinheit und Glaube webt sie beständig neu
lässt uns zueinander finden ohne jede Scheu.

Das Lachen, das aus dem Herzen sich drängt
hat sich in unsere Seelen gemengt
es ist wie eine neue Lebensenergie
ich frage mich nur, wie machst du das, wie?

So find ich dich überall, im Schlaf und im Traum
die Liebe im Herzen schafft unendlichen Raum,
sie lebt und atmet und drängt sich zum Licht
und kommt ganz von Gott, vergiss das bitte nicht.

don't be silly you lilly
there is nothing to fear
I guess you don't know
that I like you to be here

the sun will shine brighter
the stars will bend low
just listen and watch
and stay in the flow

so keep up the spirit
let life flow and love
nothing will ever be broken
light is shining from above

the lows of life
are passing and gone
nothing really counts
as only the ONE.

Die Stille des Einsseins
schafft Raum
für den Traum

Die Weite des Seins
öffnet Verstand
und Herz

Willst du vertrauen
so umarme
den Schmerz

Willst du fröhlich sein
so öffne
dein Herz.

No matter what
the world still turns and turns
no matter what
my heart still aches and burns

it wants you
it needs you
is it calling in vain
or is it really
just a game.

if real love enters
the rules might be changed
if not - I am sorry
maybe even the writing
is in vain.

es steckt ein lied in allen dingen
sei still und hör gut zu,
es klingt magie im herzen
bist du nur wirklich du
die antwort ist die liebe
die in uns allen wohnt,
und jeder der nun höret,
find't in sich innere ruh.

And when we meet again
the spirit will be bright
and thousand little stars
will dance throughout the night
love and joy will carry us
higher than high
and all we want to do is
take off and fly.

ET
28. Dez. 98

unsere seele, die wandert
wandert hin zu dem licht
sie ist dir ein freund
doch du hörst auf sie nicht

durch aeonen von welten,
meere von licht
steht sie zu diensten,
kennst du sie nicht?

sie schreit, doch du glaubst
du weißt besser als sie,
was gut ist für dich
doch niemals und nie

nie lässt du sie sein
lässt sie kommen zu wort
laberst vor dich hin,
in einem fort

da wird sie ganz still
sammelt kräfte gar viel
ist nicht mehr zu spüren
weit weg von dem ziel

der druck wird so groß
bis das licht explodiert
tausend sterne dann tanzen
in deinem leben ganz ungeniert

und plötzlich wird klar
was du immer schon weißt
die seele, die schöne
zum licht zurück reist.

do you miss flying or the magic that´s gone?
"everyday " is back and it´s hard like a bone
no freedom, no dreaming, no windy breeze
can you function like that and be at ease?

my brain, my whole body is feeling the pain,
yet I know that nothing is ever in vain
the void and the nothingness caught up with me again
and I have no idea how to handle the pain

maybe - if I really grow up - which I don´t want to do
maybe - if just for a little while I could hold on to you
maybe - life ain´t as bad as it sometimes looks
maybe - somehow I could get off the hook

everyday life and freedom - I can´t see how they fit
no answer - i ran out of my wit
I guess I just never think of it again
I just want to sleep and forget the pain.

you are like frosting on the cake
added kisses when I bake
sunrays on a diamond ring
music that I like to sing

raindrops on a day too hot
guitar strings before they pop
computer messages long or short
lots of angels coming on board

blow a whistle
sing a song
and just know
that you can do no wrong.

take the present as a present
a gift from above
a gift that is precious
and tells us of love

remember to be conscious
to see what is on
to feel what your heart says
to not be alone

the rays of sunshine
the mew of your cat
the smile someone gives you
greetings over the net

it doesn't matter
how little or big
just say thank you
nothing more to seek.

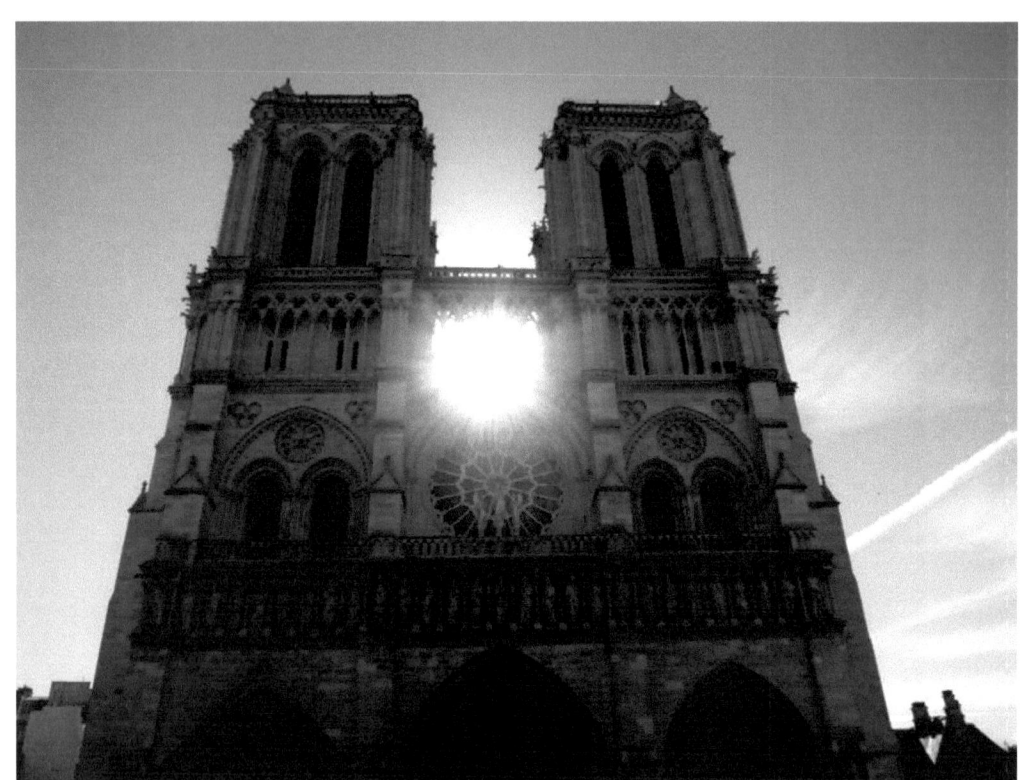

Foto

Elfi Maria Thompson was born August 15, 1947 in Leoben, Austria. She trained as a teacher and always enjoyed pushing the boundaries of what a worth-while curriculum for young learners ought to be. Before starting a family she moved to the US and by the time all her boys had flown the nest both the EU and the States had been called home at various times. After family life she returned to higher education and earned a Master's degree in Political Science at an American university. While studying she kept her artistic passion alive by writing poetry. Doing so brought a new-found depth to her relationships with friends, family and the one she loves. At present she is living in Barcelona, Spain.